4/08

COMPETITIVE
TENNIS
FOR GIRLS

JUDITH GUILLERMO-NEWTON

the rosen publishing group's
rosen central

Published in 2001 by The Rosen Publishing Group, Inc.
29 East 21st Street, New York, NY 10010

First Edition

Library of Congress Cataloging-in-Publication Data

Guillermo-Newton, Judith.
Competitive tennis for girls / by Judith Guillermo-Newton.
p. cm. — (Sportsgirl)
Includes bibliographical references (p.)
ISBN 0-8239-3407-1 (library binding)
1. Tennis—Juvenile literature. 2. Women tennis players—Juvenile literature. [1. Tennis. 2. Women tennis players.]
I. Title. II. Series.
GV996.5 .G84 2001
796.342'082—dc21
4-28-08
2001000425

Manufactured in the United States of America

Contents

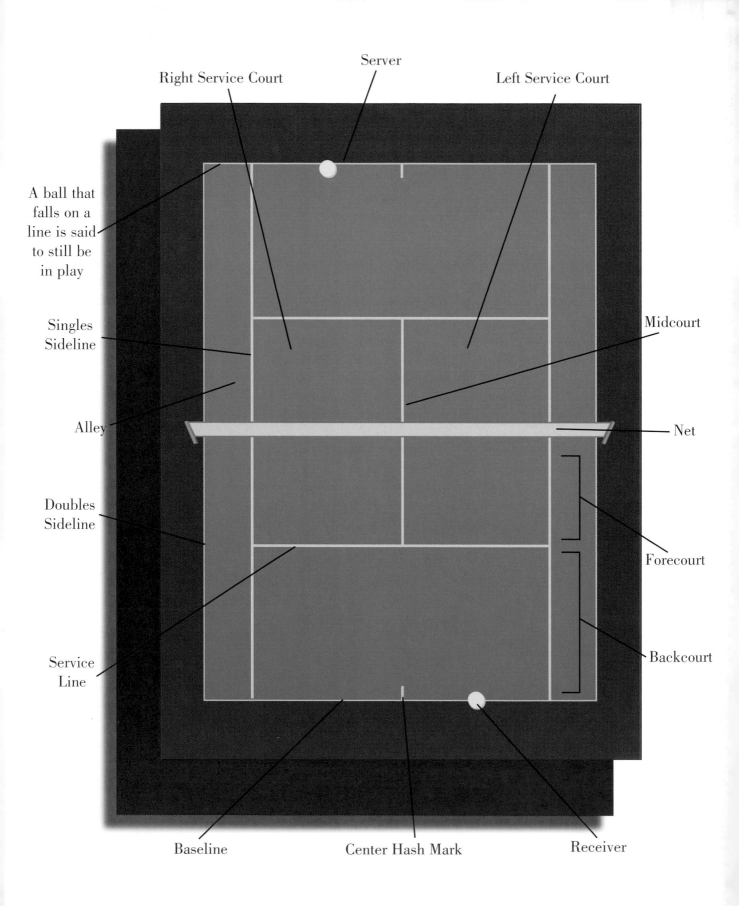

Server

Right Service Court

Left Service Court

A ball that falls on a line is said to still be in play

Singles Sideline

Midcourt

Alley

Net

Doubles Sideline

Forecourt

Backcourt

Service Line

Baseline

Center Hash Mark

Receiver

Introduction

Previous generations of women were discouraged from playing sports. Sweating, competition, and physical contact were no-no's, behaviors reserved only for boys and men. Girls and women were the ones in the stands, cheering their brothers, boyfriends, sons, and fathers on to victory.

Tremendous changes have happened for girls. All their lives, my daughters could play almost any sport they were interested in pursuing, and play with joy, without self-consciousness. I love that my daughters and all girls have this wonderful opportunity to develop their athletic selves, feel firsthand what it is like to be part of a team, and know what it takes to compete.

Tennis has been a sport that I have played for some twenty-five years. I love playing both singles and doubles, but I have grown to love doubles. I have had such fun playing with my friends, my husband, and my daughters. I regularly play on a United

Title IX prohibited discrimination against girls and women in athletic programs, greatly increasing the number of girls and women playing sports such as tennis.

States Tennis Association (USTA) team and enjoy the competition. It is wonderful to be on a team with women of all ages.

Studies show that girls benefit when they are regularly active in sports and recreational activities. These benefits include:

- They are less likely to use drugs.

- They have greater confidence, self-esteem, and pride in themselves.

- They reduce their risk of breast cancer.

- They are more likely to leave abusive relationships.

- They are less likely to get pregnant before they want to.

- They are more likely to experience academic success and graduate from high school.

The President's Council on Physical Fitness and Sports recently concluded the following:

- Girls' early involvement in physical activity and sports can reduce their likelihood of developing chronic diseases such as coronary heart disease and high cholesterol.

- Regular physical activity can help girls build greater peak bone mass, reducing the risk of osteoporosis. Exercise and sport participation gives adolescent girls positive feelings about body image, improved self-esteem, experiences of competency and success, and increased self-confidence.

In 1972, the United States Congress passed the Educational Amendments. One section of this law, Title IX, prohibits discrimination against girls and women in federally funded education, including athletic programs. The impact of Title IX on the number of girls and women playing sports has been monumental. Many more women who were under ten years old when Title IX passed play sports than those who grew up before Title IX.

Today the door is wide open for girls to experience all the wonderful benefits that occur for people lucky enough to be part of an athletic team—the fun, the work, the friendships, and the opportunity to play a sport with others who love playing as much as you do.

1 Starting Out in Tennis

Some believe that tennis is the descendant of ancient ball games played by the Egyptians, Greeks, and Romans. Others think it comes from a Roman game called harpastum, a cross between football and rugby, in which two teams fought each other to get the ball over a line marked at each end of the field. What is known, however, is that tennis has been played in England at least since the 1500s, during the reign of King Henry VIII, and was brought to the eastern United States in the late 1800s. It was often referred to as lawn tennis because matches were played on grass courts. The United States National Lawn Tennis Association formed in 1884 and that year sponsored a national championship in men's singles and doubles. In 1887, women's singles was added, and in 1890, women's doubles rounded out the tournament.

Women's tennis attire has changed dramatically throughout the years. This picture, depicting tennis enthusiasts of the day, was painted in 1887.

Tennis was then a sport of the wealthy. Like golf, it was part of the culture of private clubs that excluded African Americans, Jews, and recent immigrants. It wasn't until the mid-twentieth century that many Jewish tennis clubs and the all-black American Tennis Association were established.

Today, tennis is accessible to everyone. Over 160,000 public tennis courts exist around the United States. Some cities charge adults for public court use, but virtually all public courts are free to children. Membership in private tennis clubs is often expensive, but many clubs do have special tennis membership rates available for junior tennis players (student-age players, from eight to eighteen years old).

The equipment needed to play tennis is a tennis racket, tennis balls, tennis shoes, the use of a tennis court, and at least one other person with whom to play. In many cities there are organizations that collect used tennis rackets and make them available to beginning tennis enthusiasts. This is an excellent way to begin to play tennis and see what you think of the sport.

Tennis Equipment: The Racket and Balls

For a beginning tennis player, choosing a racket can be very confusing. The tennis racket is used to hit the ball over the net

There are many different tennis rackets on the market. Selecting one that is right for you can be challenging.

and consists of a frame, which may be of any weight, size, or shape, and stringing. It can be made of wood, graphite, titanium, or other materials.

For a beginner, the best material for stringing a racket is synthetic gut. Each manufacturer recommends the tension at which their racket is to be strung; beginners should string their rackets at the middle tension recommended. If a racket is strung too tight, it is very easy for a player to hurt her elbow. A decent beginner's racket costs about $100. A California tennis pro and

How you hold the racket is important, so choose a racket that you can grip comfortably.

shop owner warns, "The cheaper tennis rackets are generally heavier and less forgiving. They make it harder for a beginner to learn the game."

A shop specializing in tennis equipment can help you decide which racket is best for you. In choosing a racket, it is vital to get the correct grip (handle) size. To determine grip size, take the racket by the end of the handle as if you were going to shake hands. Close your fingers around the grip; there should be one finger's width of space between your thumb and index finger.

To play tennis, you also need a can of balls. Tennis balls are usually sold three to a can. Most tennis balls are yellow or white, and they are made up of a pressurized rubber core covered with high-quality cloth, usually wool mixed with nylon. With play, tennis balls gradually go soft and need to be replaced. When tennis balls go soft, they're referred to as dead balls. Playing with dead balls can cause you to injure your elbow.

Tennis Attire

Most public courts do not have a strict dress code. The only rule usually refers to tennis shoes; players must use soft-sole rubber shoes that do not leave marks on the court surface. This usually means no black-sole tennis shoes. Playing tennis can be hard on your feet. Good tennis shoes are essential for preventing injuries because they support the foot and absorb shock. There are shoes designed especially for tennis, but if you play only occasionally, or play several sports, you can use a pair of cross-trainers.

Private tennis courts very often have specific dress codes. This often means all white clothes, tennis skirts for women,

Women's tennis has come a long way in a short time. Notice the contrast between 1922's Suzanne Lenglen (*left*) and Billie Jean King, who is pictured winning Wimbledon in 1966.

and tennis shorts for men. Many tennis clubs today allow their members to wear colored tennis clothing. It is a good idea to check if the court on which you are playing has a dress code.

The Tennis Court

The dimensions of a tennis court are seventy-eight feet by twenty-seven feet for singles (one-on-one play) and seventy-eight feet by thirty-six feet for doubles (when teams of two play one another). The net, located midcourt, is three feet high in the center. At each side where it is supported by posts, the net stands three and a half feet high. Although grass courts are still in use, the most common court materials today are clay, cement, and a number of cushioned asphalt and synthetic surfaces. These are usually referred to as hard courts.

If you are playing doubles, you use the entire width of the tennis court. If you are playing singles, the inside vertical line, or alley line, designates your court (see illustration on page 4). The service line is the horizontal line eighteen feet from the back line of the court (the baseline). It is the start of the service court. The service court is divided in the center into right and left service courts. The area between the service line and the baseline is referred to as the backcourt.

The Strange Scoring System of Tennis

To win a tennis game, a player must win four points and win by a margin of two. The scoring progresses: 15, 30, 40, and game. If you are tied at 40-40, this is called deuce. If the server wins the next point, the score is referred to as advantage-in, or ad-in. If she wins the next point, the server wins by two points, and the game is over. If the receiver wins the next point after deuce, the score is advantage-out, or ad-out. One always has to win by two points for the game to be over. There is no limit to the number of deuce points that can be played in a game.

To win a tennis match, a player must win two out of three sets.

When calling out the score, the server's score is always reported first: the score 30-15 means that the server has won two points and the receiver has won one. One person serves an entire game. In tennis, zero is generally referred to as "love," from the French word *l'oeuf*, which means "egg." The score love-40 tells us the server has no points and the receiver has three.

A player loses the point by missing the ball, hitting it into the net, or hitting it out of bounds. A server loses the point immediately if she commits a double fault, failing to hit the ball in the service box after two tries.

As points make up a game, games make up a set, and sets make up a match. The first player to win six games wins the set, although a player must be two games ahead to win—a set could be won at 7-5. If the set score ends at 6-6, the players either play a tiebreaker or continue to play until one person is ahead by two games. To win a match, a player must win two out of three sets. In a limited number of tournaments, a match consists of five sets, the winner winning three out of five.

The Serve

For most beginning players, the serve is the most difficult and frustrating tennis skill to learn. This is the shot used by players to begin a point. The actual motion used to hit the ball is referred to as the service motion. To be a legitimate serve, the tennis ball must cross the net without touching it, and land crosscourt in the service box on the opposite side of the net. If the ball touches the net and bounces into the service box, this is called a let, and the server gets another try. The server is allowed two tries to get the ball legally into play. If a ball does not land in the server's box, this is called a fault. If she is not successful on either attempt, this is called a double fault and she loses the point.

Service starts on the right side of the court (the deuce court). The server must stand behind the baseline anywhere between the center hash mark and the alley line. After the point is completed, the server moves to the left side of the court (the ad court) and serves diagonally across the court once again.

Venus Williams is the strongest server in women's tennis today.

The young lady in the far court prepares to hit a volley.
Note how she stands close to the net with her feet spread apart.

Ground Strokes

A ground stroke is a tennis stroke generally hit by a player from the baseline. When both players stand at or behind the baseline to hit balls back and forth to one another, this is a baseline rally.

The forehand is one of two basic ground strokes. If a player is right-handed and hits the ball on her right side, this tennis stroke is called a forehand. If the player is left-handed and hits the ball on her left side, this is her forehand. The ball strikes the racket on the front of the strings.

Forehand Tips

Always pull the racket back as soon as the ball is approaching your forehand side.

Try to hit the ball on the sweet spot (middle area) of the racket.

When hitting the ball, keep your feet spread about shoulder-width apart.

Step toward the ball with your right foot if you're right-handed, your left foot if you're left-handed.

Continue your stroke after you've hit the ball so that your racket head follows through the ball toward your opposite shoulder.

Backhand Tips

As the ball is hit toward you, turn your shoulders to the left if you are right-handed, to the right if you are left-handed. Your back will be to the net.

When hitting the ball, keep your head very still. Follow the ball with your eyes only.

When hitting the ball, keep your feet spread about shoulder-width apart.

Finish the two-handed shot up and over the right shoulder (opposite if you are left-handed).

The backhand, in which the ball hits the backside of the tennis racket, is the other basic ground stroke of tennis. If a player is right-handed, a ball hit on the left side of her body would be a backhand. (The reverse is true for left-handers.) To hit the ball, she has to cross her body with the hand holding the racket. Much more commonly than in the forehand stroke, the backhand can be hit with one or two hands holding the racket.

The Volley

The volley is a type of tennis shot made while the player is standing close to the net. With a short, punching motion, the player tries to hit the ball in the air before it bounces. When hitting a volley, the player wants to stand about three feet from the net with her feet spread apart about shoulder-width. The racket strings should be perpendicular to the ground and the racket should be directly in front of her. The bottom of the handle should be even with the belly button. When the ball crosses the net, the player wants to meet it with a short jab-like stroke.

Tennis Lessons

Tennis is a game in which receiving formal lessons can be extremely helpful, both in learning the game and continuing to improve. It is very easy to develop bad habits that can limit your progress as well as potentially cause you tennis injuries.

A tennis pro can teach you tips and tricks and help you "unlearn" bad habits that you may have picked up while playing.

Good tennis instruction is available from many different places. The YMCA and most public tennis courts or city recreation programs offer affordable tennis lessons. Group tennis lessons are the least expensive way to get formal instruction. This is also an easy way to meet other people, at your level, with whom to play tennis. Private tennis clubs and private professionals also offer tennis instruction, but the cost is usually much higher than public recreation programs.

Private lessons, where a player can work one-on-one with a tennis instructor, are the best way to get good individual attention. The United States Tennis Association (USTA) offers many tennis programs in different areas around the country. They are easily accessed through the Internet at www.USTA.com. In *Tennis* magazine, put out by the USTA, there is a list of many different tennis camps available throughout the world.

2 Preparing to Play Tennis: Training

Aerobic activities, strength training, and stretching will get a person in the necessary condition for tennis. Tennis is a game of quick motions, stopping and starting, and sudden surges at maximum speed. Playing tennis improves flexibility in the joints, primarily in the hips and the shoulders, which are used in the serving motion. Tennis also develops and tones one's muscles, especially the arms, calves, hamstrings, quadriceps, shoulders, and upper back. All players will improve their cardiovascular fitness, but as one's skill level improves, workouts become more intense, partly because the points take longer to play. As players improve, they can move their opponents around the court more, which also makes tennis an active aerobic workout.

Footwork is important in tennis, so any physical activity that concentrates on and helps your footwork would be an asset to your tennis game. Soccer and tennis

A good warm-up is to stand near the net and gently hit the ball back and forth to your tennis partner or a friend.

are very complementary sports. Soccer emphasizes foot coordination, anticipation, and placement, helpful skills for tennis. Playing another sport also helps you not to burn out on tennis, a problem for many young athletes who focus on just one sport. Playing more than one sport also allows your body time to recover and rest, as well as reduces the problems associated with overuse and repetitive motion.

The Warm-up

The more fit you are, the better your chances of reducing the risk of injury. It is very important to warm up for five to ten minutes before playing tennis; this small amount of effort can greatly reduce your chances of getting hurt. A good warm-up is to come to the net and gently hit the ball back and forth to one another. This should get your muscles warm and your eyes focusing on the ball. As your muscles get loose, you can then move to the baseline and hit ground strokes.

Be sure to stretch the major muscle groups after you warm up to prevent injury. Stretch again after playing tennis to promote flexibility and prevent unnecessary soreness. The muscles you should concentrate on warming up are the calves, gluteus muscles, hamstrings, quadriceps, shoulders, triceps, and upper and lower back.

To boost your agility, try running sideways from sideline to sideline, sprinting forward from the baseline to the net, and running backward from the net back to the baseline. To work on your hand-eye coordination, practice hitting against a backboard or with a ball machine, or play softball, Ping-Pong, racketball, or squash. Also work on strengthening your arms and lower back, two of the areas most often injured in tennis.

Tennis Injuries

A crucial reason to take tennis lessons is that learning the proper way to hit a stroke is the best insurance you can have against injury. Warming up and stretching both before and after you play tennis also helps. The most common tennis injuries are to the feet, ankles, knees, elbows, and shoulders.

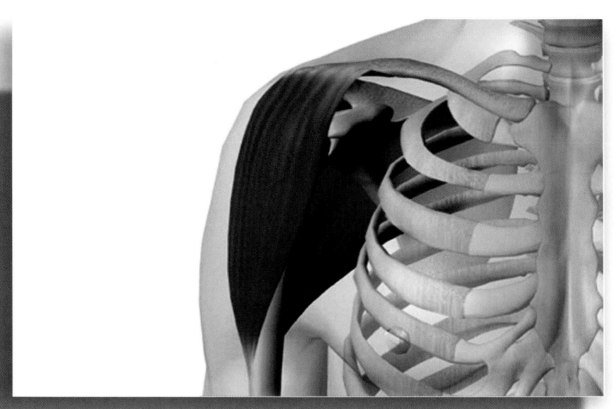

When you serve a tennis ball, you use the following: the deltoid muscle, a triangular, three-part muscle that wraps around the top of your shoulder, and the rotator cuff, a set of four small muscles connecting your shoulder and upper arm.

The feet probably take more abuse than any other part of the human body. They not only support our entire body, they also act as shock absorbers. The feet are also responsible for keeping our bodies balanced as we quickly stop and start on the tennis court. Our side-to-side movement and the hard surfaces of the tennis court are also fatiguing to our feet. Injured feet can also contribute to ankle and knee injuries.

Properly fitting tennis shoes are absolutely essential for keeping your feet in good shape. They not only offer arch support, they also help absorb the pounding you get from playing on hard courts. The fit of your shoes is important because excessive friction between the shoe and the skin can cause blisters. Thin socks or ones that don't breathe can also cause blisters. Poorly-fitting footwear can also cause calluses to form on your feet. Calluses are thick, hardened patches of dead skin cells that form over areas of bone pressure, usually on the ball or heel of the foot. For people who have weak ankles, high-top tennis shoes can be helpful in preventing injuries.

An alarming number of female athletes, 30,000 each year, are reporting injuries to their knees' anterior cruciate ligaments, or ACL, the elastic-like bands that connect the shins and thigh bones. Researchers say running backward can help build hamstring muscles. Bending the knees when playing tennis can also help reduce ACL injuries.

The most common cause of elbow pain in tennis players is a tendon problem. In fact, it is so common that it's called tennis elbow. The usual causes are poor technique, most commonly on your backhand stroke, or using a racket with the wrong grip size. This is yet another reason to have a tennis professional help you choose the proper racket and teach you how to correctly hit a ball.

The serving motion especially involves the muscles in the shoulder. The most important muscles in your shoulder are the deltoid muscle, a triangular, three-part muscle that wraps around the top of the shoulder, and the rotator cuff, a set of four small muscles connecting your shoulder and upper arm. All of these muscles are used when serving a tennis ball.

Overuse of the shoulder is common in tennis. Doing proper strengthening exercises can help prevent this injury as well as improve your serve. Good flexibility will help minimize muscle tears when going for hard-to-reach shots. Shoulder and chest muscles can be stretched easily using a towel or racket. Stretches should be done slowly and held for ten seconds.

Again, proper technique is the best way to combat shoulder injury. When you serve, how you throw your toss, the ball's height and placement, can dictate the stress placed on your shoulder. The actual service motion, the movement with your racket, is also important. To prevent future problems, have a tennis pro review your stroke.

Aerobic activities, strength training, and stretching will get you in the necessary condition for tennis. Running, swimming, bicycling, kickboxing, or any aerobic work-out is good cross training for tennis players. It is important to have stamina in order to play tennis matches. In the end, the outcomes of many matches are decided not by a player's tennis ability,

Use a towel or your racket to stretch your shoulder and chest muscles.

Swimming is a good cross-training exercise for tennis players.

but rather by which player is in better physical condition. Regular aerobic exercise will help your overall physical state.

No workout program would be complete without strength training. You need to do resistance training to maintain and improve your muscular strength and endurance, boost your metabolism, and strengthen your bones.

Weight training increases your muscular strength and mass. Many girls are worried that they will look too muscular if they lift weights. Muscle takes up less space than fat, so you can look trimmer even if your weight increases. Recent studies have found that strength training can lift people's spirits and help them sleep better.

"I always wanted to be somebody. If I made it, it's half because I was game enough to take a lot of punishment along the way and half because there were a lot of people who cared enough to help me."—Althea Gibson

Althea Gibson

National and international tennis champion Althea Gibson challenged both other tennis athletes and the racial segregation of tennis that was part of our country's social structure in the 1950s.

Born to sharecropper parents in South Carolina on August 27, 1927, the African American Gibson grew up in poverty in Harlem. She loved most sports but adored tennis. In 1942, when Gibson was fifteen years old, she won the girls' singles event at the American Tennis Association's New York State Tournament. The ATA was an all-black tennis organization, since African Americans were not allowed to take part in tournaments with white players.

But Althea Gibson would not be discouraged. In 1951, she became the first African American of either sex to be allowed to enter the Forest Hills National Grass Court Championship. She later went on to win Forest Hills, Wimbledon, and the French Open.

Althea Gibson is a woman of much success, courage, and perseverance. Along with her athletic achievements, Gibson should also be recognized as the first African American of either sex to break the color barrier in national and international tournament tennis.

Billie Jean King is one of the greatest tennis players of all time, among both women and men.

Billie Jean King

Billie Jean (Moffitt) King was born in Long Beach, California, on November 22, 1943. She has done more for women's tennis than any other player.

King won her first of twenty Wimbledon titles in 1961. She captured six singles, ten doubles, and four mixed titles. Additionally, she has thirteen U.S. Open victories, a French Open title, and an Australian Open title. With twenty-seven major doubles titles, she has been credited with being one of the greatest doubles players in the history of tennis.

In 1971, King was the first woman athlete to win more than $100,000 in one season. Her much-publicized Battle of the Sexes match against male tennis player Bobby Riggs set a record for the largest tennis audience and the largest prize awarded up to that time. And Billie Jean won!

Billie Jean King worked relentlessly for the rights of women players, cofounding the Women's Tennis Association (WTA) in 1974. She retired from competitive tennis in 1984 and became the first woman commissioner in professional sports. Many of the opportunities open to young women athletes today can be credited to the work done by Billie Jean King.

3

It's Only a Sport: Looking at Competition

We've all seen the classic "poor sport" on the tennis court—the girl who throws her racket when she makes an error, constantly argues with the lineperson about calls, uses bad language, or cheats to win a game. Many athletes let competition take the fun out of the sport. It is important to remember that when we try our hardest and we lose, we are not losers—we merely lost a game.

Tennis is as much a game of the mind as it is of the body. The mental game consists of staying focused and not getting distracted. It means talking positively to yourself and staying composed even when things are not working in your favor. It means forgiving yourself when you make a mistake and encouraging yourself to do better.

Monica Seles, a professional tennis player who has been the number one player in the world, is a great role model for

When asked about the importance of mental toughness, Steffi Graf replied, "Very important. I mean, it is mental toughness, confidence, and to really have your game together. These components are the most important."

mental toughness. She has won some of the most prestigious tennis tournaments in the world: the French Open, the U.S. Open, and the Australian Open. She has won some of these more than one time. When you see her on the court, you can feel Seles's intensity of focus. Nothing distracts her; she is completely in the moment, paying attention only to herself and her task at hand. In an interview after the 2000 U.S. Open, Seles said, "When I go out there and play, I try to be so focused. If I'm not, I'm in deep trouble for my style of game and my personality."

Another woman tennis player who possesses amazing mental toughness is Steffi Graf. Another champion, Tracy Austin, says of Graf, "Her mental toughness puts her right up there with the Michael Jordans, the Wayne Gretzkys, and the John Elways."

Few players thrive on negativity or pressure. The key is to have fun. Approach problems as a puzzle you can enjoy solving. Look for patterns. Try new things if what you are doing is not working. Don't let adversity get the better of you. Give your very best, but look at your losses as learning experiences. Many coaches say they learn more from their losses than they do from their wins. Most important, believe in yourself; see yourself as a winner, both on and off the court. Remember that self-esteem comes from working at something and getting better at it. Allow playing tennis to enhance your self-esteem, not destroy it.

The idea of competition can be difficult for many girls. Some of us are uncomfortable with the idea that girls can be as competitive as boys. We see it as a "male thing." But

Self-esteem comes from working hard at something, such as a sport, and getting better at it.

many girls love to compete; they are driven by the idea of excelling and of winning. They want to be the best at whatever it is they are doing, be it tennis, soccer, dance, or debate. They receive great pleasure from entering the competition, challenging others, and seeing themselves succeed. You can be a passionate competitor, especially in sports, and not have to apologize for it.

For those who aren't competitive by nature, remember that it is okay to win. If you beat someone else, it does not make you a bad person. Shape competition into a game in which the goal is to give your personal best regardless of the result.

"In the '70s, many of us, myself included, were outrageous and cutting-edge. But in my generation we also tried to please. In the '90s, these young women certainly are showing their self-confidence. If they had been boys or young men, everyone would have expected it. It's a fine line, but I like the fact that these girls have higher self-esteem and they're not afraid to show it."

—Billie Jean King

There are some sports that are referred to as so-called body sports, in which a girl's body seems on display. This includes tennis. Girls who play these sports are most at risk for eating disorders. It is important to fuel your body properly. You work it hard when you train and play, and, like any machine, your body must be well maintained if it's to operate at its best. Eating well-balanced meals, drinking plenty of water, and getting enough sleep are important.

In her book, *Embracing Victory*, Mariah Burton Nelson, an award-winning author and athlete, offers a view of competition she refers to as a partnership model. Nelson looks at power not as "power over" (dominating power) but as "power to" (power as competence). She sees teammates, coaches, and even opposing

Winning isn't everything, but if you are a competitive
person, it can make you feel great.

players viewing each other as comrades rather than enemies. She proposes that these "comrades" help us to find the best in ourselves by challenging us and pushing us to do better.

Nelson also talks about the need for women to feel comfortable about taking up space with their bodies and their voices, conveying their ideas, asserting their own needs, and refusing to shrink to meet someone's approval.

In 1994, a survey by *Women's Sport and Fitness* magazine found that 82 percent of the most powerful women in Washington politics played organized sports when young.

4 Tennis: A Game of a Lifetime

There are thousands of players all over the country participating in tennis camps, events, and tournaments for men and women of all ages. The United States Tennis Association has many leagues for competitive tennis. There are even official USTA tournaments for players in their eighties and nineties.

There are many junior programs all over the world that sponsor tennis tournaments, lessons, clinics, and camps for boys and girls ages eight to eighteen. The USTA has a competitive league called Junior Team Tennis. Junior Team Tennis is a fun way to meet other kids and play matches against one another. Many city recreation departments and YMCAs also have junior tennis leagues.

Thanks to Title IX, today you can visit almost any high school in the United States and find a girls' tennis

When Lindsay Davenport was a child, no one expected her to be America's next great tennis player. Here she is at the U.S. Open, the first woman born in the United States to win since Chris Evert in 1982.

team. Just as in other sports, girls' tennis teams compete against teams from other schools in their division. A high school tennis team is usually composed of girls who compete in either singles or doubles play.

Many players decide that they would like to play tennis in college. Again, because of Title IX, there are many girls' tennis teams found on college and university campuses. If a girl played tennis well enough in high school, she may even attend college on a sports scholarship.

The level of coaching and playing ability varies from school to school. Southern California schools, for instance, employ strong coaches. Tennis professionals such as Lindsay Davenport and Tracy Austin participated on their high school tennis teams in southern California. In other areas of the country, tennis is not as competitive a sport, making it easier to earn a spot on high school tennis teams.

The schools in the National Collegiate Athletic Association (NCAA) are classified into three divisions. The most competitive teams are in Division One. There are a number of other college athletic associations, such as the National Association of Intercollegiate Athletics (NAIA) and the New England Small College Athletic Conference (NESCAC). The NESCAC's mission statement says that it is "committed first and foremost to academic excellence and believes that athletic excellence supports our educational mission."

Thanks to pioneers like Billie Jean King, professional women's tennis can be both an athletically and a financially rewarding profession. In 1974, Chris Evert was the first woman to make over a million dollars playing professional tennis. Today, most of the top women tennis professionals are multimillionaires.

On the recreational level, tennis is a wonderful way to make friends and stay in good physical condition. You can see entire families playing tennis together, couples enjoying themselves playing mixed doubles, and friends of many different ages joining USTA leagues. Tennis is truly a sport of a lifetime.

Playing tennis is a great way to stay in shape, learn self-discipline, and make new friends.

1881
The U.S. Champion Tennis Tournament begins. In 1968, the name of the tournament is changed to the U.S. Open.

1916
The American Tennis Association is formed. This is the oldest black sports organization in the United States.

1947
Althea Gibson wins the first of ten consecutive American Tennis Association national championships.

1953
Maureen "Little Mo" Connolly, age sixteen, becomes the first woman to score a Grand Slam.

1971
The Association for Intercollegiate Athletics for Women is formed.

1884
Women's events are added to the Wimbledon tennis tournament.

1935
The U.S. Championship Tennis Tournament officially includes women.

1971
Billie Jean King becomes the first female athlete to win more than $100,000 in a single season in any sport.

1927
Helen Wills Moody is the first American woman to win Wimbledon.

1951
Althea Gibson becomes the first African American to enter Wimbledon. She would win Wimbledon twice.

1956
Althea Gibson wins the French Open, becoming the first African American to win a Grand Slam singles title.

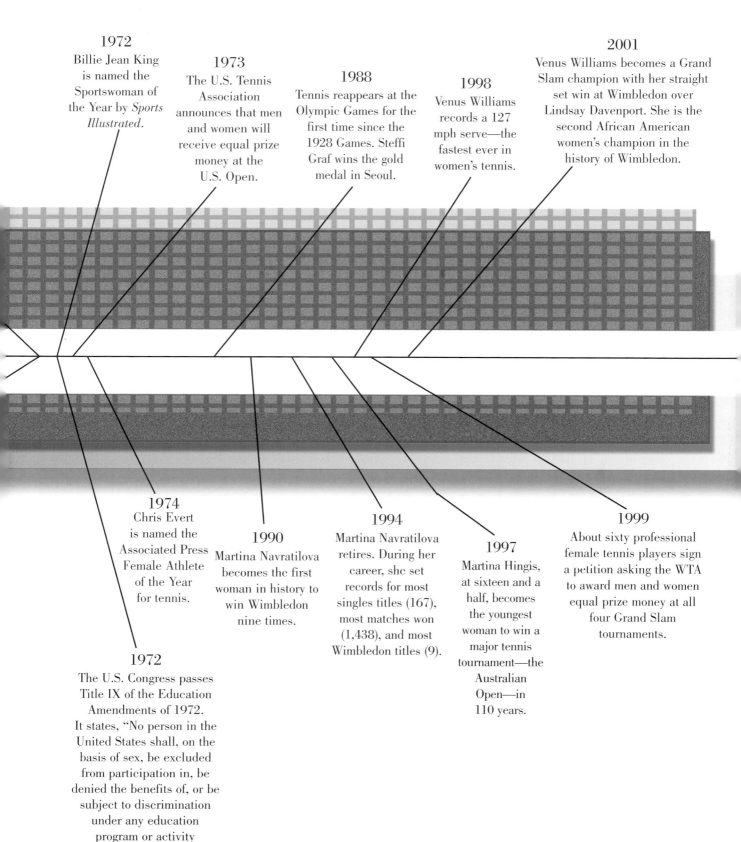

1972
Billie Jean King is named the Sportswoman of the Year by *Sports Illustrated*.

1973
The U.S. Tennis Association announces that men and women will receive equal prize money at the U.S. Open.

1988
Tennis reappears at the Olympic Games for the first time since the 1928 Games. Steffi Graf wins the gold medal in Seoul.

1998
Venus Williams records a 127 mph serve—the fastest ever in women's tennis.

2001
Venus Williams becomes a Grand Slam champion with her straight set win at Wimbledon over Lindsay Davenport. She is the second African American women's champion in the history of Wimbledon.

1974
Chris Evert is named the Associated Press Female Athlete of the Year for tennis.

1990
Martina Navratilova becomes the first woman in history to win Wimbledon nine times.

1994
Martina Navratilova retires. During her career, she set records for most singles titles (167), most matches won (1,438), and most Wimbledon titles (9).

1997
Martina Hingis, at sixteen and a half, becomes the youngest woman to win a major tennis tournament—the Australian Open—in 110 years.

1999
About sixty professional female tennis players sign a petition asking the WTA to award men and women equal prize money at all four Grand Slam tournaments.

1972
The U.S. Congress passes Title IX of the Education Amendments of 1972. It states, "No person in the United States shall, on the basis of sex, be excluded from participation in, be denied the benefits of, or be subject to discrimination under any education program or activity receiving Federal financial assistance."

Tennis Terms

advantage (ad) court   The right side service box.

approach shot   The transition shot that allows a player to get from the baseline area to the net. This can be hit off the forehand and backhand sides.

center hash mark   A line that divides each side of the court in half and is crucial to the serving game.

changeover   Players must change ends of the court when the games add up to an odd number. This keeps the match fair so that both players must face elements such as the wind, sun, and shade.

deuce court The left side service box. The first point of every competitive game starts in the deuce court.

doubles alley Long, narrow rectangles created by the singles and doubles sidelines running parallel with each other. These alleys are used only in doubles play.

down the line Down one of the sidelines. A shot down the line is a lower percentage shot because the net is higher and the ball doesn't travel as far.

first serve At the beginning of each point, the server has two chances to get the serve in. The first serve is usually the harder serve.

foot fault The server cannot touch or cross the baseline with either foot before the ball is hit. If this occurs, it is called a foot fault.

let A first or second serve that hits the net and lands in the service box. The serve must be taken over.

return of serve The shot made by a player when receiving the serve.

tiebreaker At 6-all in games, in any given set, players must play a tiebreaker. The first player to reach 7 by a margin of 2 is the winner. The points are counted as 1, 2, 3 . . . and so on. A tiebreaker can go on until someone eventually wins by two points, such as 18-16.

winning the toss   One player spins her racket or tosses a coin to see who gets choice of serve or side of the court, not both. If you choose to serve, then the opponent chooses which side of the court she wants first.

Glossary

ace   A legal serve that does not touch the receiver's racket.

advantage   The next point calling deuce. If the server wins the point, it is called advantage in; if the receiver wins, it is called advantage out. Also referred to as the ad point.

alley line   Inside vertical line on the tennis court; designates singles court.

backcourt   The area between the service line and the baseline.

backhand   A tennis stroke in which the ball is hit with the back side of the racket. The shoulder of the arm holding the racket faces the net before bringing the racket forward and across the body to meet the ball. If a player is right-handed, a shot hit on the left side of the player's body would be her backhand. For a left-hander, it would be a shot hit on her right side.

baseline   The line at the back of the court.

baseline rally   When both players stand at or behind the baseline to hit the ball back and forth to each other.

break   When the receiver wins the game, this is a service break.

crosscourt   When a player hits the ball diagonally across the court, over the net. This is the highest percentage shot you can hit because the ball has to travel over the lowest part of the net for the longest distance on the court.

deuce   Tied score of 40-40. Because a game must be won by two points, play continues until one player leads by a margin of two points.

double fault   Two consecutive serving errors that result in the loss of a point.

forehand   A tennis stroke in which the player pivots her body so that the shoulder of the arm not holding the racket faces the net. The player then swings the racket forward to meet the ball. The ball is hit on the right side on a player if she is right-handed, and the left side if she is left-handed.

game   A tennis game is composed of at least four points. The winner must win by a margin of two points.

grip   The handle of the racket; also refers to the way a player holds the racket in her hand.

groundstroke   A tennis stroke generally hit by a player from the baseline.

hard court   Any tennis court that is made from an asphalt derivative or synthetic surface.

love   Term for a score of zero. This can pertain to points, games, and sets.

net   Divides the entire court in half and is supported by netposts. There is usually a center net strap that can be adjusted to maintain regulation height. The net should be thirty-six inches high at the center of the strap.

points, games, sets, and matches   Points make up games, games make up sets, and sets make up matches. When a player wins four points by a margin of two, she has won a game. When a player wins six games (with the exception of 5-all and 6-all) she has won a set. Most matches are best of three tiebreak sets. Someone must win two out of three sets to win the match. In some tournaments, men must win three out of five sets to win the match.

rally   A series of shots hit back and forth between two players.

receiver   The player who receives the serve.

serve   Begins every point of a tennis match. A player is allowed two tries to make a legal serve.

service box   The rectangular area in which a legal serve must land. Also referred to as the service court.

service line   The horizontal line eighteen feet from the baseline. It is the start of the service court.

volley   A shot made before the ball bounces; often used by the player at the net.

warm-up   The time prior to a game in which players hit the ball back and forth.

For More Information

In the United States

United States Tennis Association (USTA)
P.O. Box 5046
White Plains, NY 10602-5046
(800) 990-USTA (8782)
e-mail: memberservices@usta.com
Web site: http://www.USTA.com

Women's Sports Foundation (WSF)
Eisenhower Park
East Meadow, NY 11554
(516) 542-4700
(800) 227-3988
Web site: http://
        www.womenssportsfoundation.org

In Canada

TennisCanada
National Tennis Centre
3111 Steeles Avenue West
Downsview, ON M3J 3H2
(416) 665-9777
Web site: http://www.tenniscanada.com

Magazines

Tennis Magazine
(800) 666-8336
Web site: http://www.tennis.com

Web Sites

Tennis.com
http://www.tennis.com

Women's Tennis Association Tour
http://www.wtatour.com

For Further Reading

Brewer, Lewis. *Professional Tennis Drills: 75 Drills to Perfect Your Strokes, Footwork, Conditioning, Court Movement, and Strategy.* New York: Scribner's, 1985.

Gallwey, W. Timothy. *The Inner Game of Tennis.* Rev. ed. New York: Random House, 1997.

Hastings, Penny, and Todd Caven. *How to Win a Sports Scholarship.* 2nd ed. Los Angeles: First Base Sports, 1999.

Hastings, Penny. *Sports for Her: A Reference Guide for Teenage Girls.* Westport, CT: Greenwood Publishing Group, 1999.

Heywood, Leslie. *Pretty Good for a Girl: An Athlete's Story.* Minneapolis, MN: University of Minnesota Press, 2000.

Lamott, Anne. *Crooked Little Heart*. New York: Anchor Books, 1998.

Macy, Sue, and Jane Gottesman, eds. *Play Like a Girl: A Celebration of Women in Sports*. New York: Henry Holt and Co., 1999.

Miles, Ellen. *Superstars of Women's Tennis*. New York: Aladdin Paperbacks, 2000.

Nelson, Mariah Burton. *Are We Winning Yet? How Women Are Changing Sports and Sports Are Changing Women*. New York: Random House, 1991.

Nelson, Mariah Burton. *Embracing Victory: Life Lessons in Competition and Compassion*. New York: William Morrow and Company, Inc., 1998.

Roetert, Paul, and Todd Ellenbecker, eds. *Complete Conditioning for Tennis*. Champaign, IL: Human Kinetics Publishers, 1998.

Rutledge, Rachel. *The Best of the Best in Tennis*. Brookfield, CT: Millbrook Press, 1998.

Silby, Caroline, and Shelley Smith. *Games Girls Play: Understanding and Guiding Young Female Athletes*. New York: St. Martin's Press, 2000.

Stewart, Mark. *Monica Seles: The Comeback Kid*. New York: The Children's Press, 1997.

USTA Staff. *Guide for Prospective Tennis Players*. White Plains, NY: United States Tennis Association, 1998.

Index

R

racket, composition/elements of,
    11–13
  grip, 12–13, 29
  tension, 12
Riggs, Bobby, 35

S

Seles, Monica, 36–38
self-confidence, 7
self-esteem, 6, 7, 38
serve, 17, 30
service box, 16, 17
service court, 15
service line, 15
service motion, 17, 25, 29, 30
shoulder injuries, 27, 29–30
sports, benefits of, 6–7
strength training, 25, 30, 31
stretching, 25, 27, 30

T

team, being part of a, 5, 6, 8
tennis
  attire, 13–14
  camps, 24, 43
  court, dimensions/areas of,
    14–15
  equipment needed for, 11–13
  history of, 9–10
  injuries, 12, 13, 22, 26, 27–31
  lessons, 22–24, 43

physical benefits of, 25
scoring of, 15–17
training for, 25–26, 27, 30–31
tennis elbow, 29
Tennis magazine, 24
tennis shoes, 11, 13, 28–29

U

United States National Lawn Tennis
    Association, 9
United States Tennis Association
    (USTA), 5–6, 22–24, 43, 46
U.S. Open, 35, 38

V

volley, 19–22

W

warming up, 26–27
weight training, 31
Wimbledon, 33, 35
Women's Sport and Fitness
    magazine, 42
Women's Tennis Association
    (WTA), 35

Y

YMCAs, 22, 43

About the Author

Judith Guillermo-Newton is a psychotherapist who lives in Santa Barbara, Calfornia. She has been a recreational tennis player for twenty-five years and plays on a USTA tennis team. She is the mother of two daughters, both of whom played on their high school varsity tennis teams. In addition to her private practice, she works at the University of California Santa Barbara Women's Center as the coordinator of the sexual harassment prevention education program for the campus. She is also responsible for coordinating the UCSB campus celebration of National Girls and Women Sports Day.

Photo Credits

Cover and photos on pp. 3, 11, 12, 16, 19, 20, 23, 26, 30, 39, 40, 41, 47, 50, 53, 57, 59, 61 by Maura Burochow; ball on cover and pp. 5, 6, 9, 10, 13, 25, 36, 43 © Corbis; p. 14 © Allsport/Hulton Deutsch (left), © Allsport (right); p. 18 © Allsport; p. 28 © Life Art; p. 31 © FPG International; p. 32 © Bettmann/Corbis; p. 34 © Tony Duffy/Allsport; p. 37 © AP/Worldwide; p. 44 © AFP/Corbis. Diagrams on pp. 4, 48–49 by Tom Forget.

Special thanks to Cardinal Gibbons High School in Fort Lauderdale, Florida.

Series Design

Danielle Goldblatt

Layout

Claudia Carlson